WRITING TOASTS & SPEECHES

*Finding
the Perfect
Words*

JO PACKHAM

A Sterling\Chapelle Book
Sterling Publishing Co., Inc. New York

Jo Packham, author
Tina Annette Brady, designer
Sandra Durbin Chapman, editor
Margaret Shields Marti, editor

The author would like to thank the following for permission to reprint:

The Toastmaster's Treasure Chest by Herbert V. Prochman and Herbert V. Prochman, Jr. Copyright © 1979 by Harper & Row. Reprinted by permission of HarperCollins Publishers.

Letters to Karen by Charles W. Shedd. Reprinted by permission of Abington Press.

Library of Congress Cataloging-in-Publication Data
Packham, Jo.
    Wedding toasts & speeches : finding the perfect words / Jo Packham
    p. ; cm.
    "A Sterling/Chapelle book"
    Includes index
    ISBN 0-8069-8832-0
    1.Toasts. 2. Public Speaking. 3. Weddings—Quotations, maxims,
etc. I. Title. II. Title: Wedding toasts and speeches.
 PN6341.P33   1993
808.5'1—dc20

Published in paperback in 2007 by Sterling Publishing Company, Inc.
387 Park Avenue South, New York, NY 10016
© 1993 by Chapelle Ltd.
Distributed in Canada by Sterling Publishing
c/o Canadian Manda Group, 165 Dufferin Street
Toronto, Ontario, Canada M6K 3H6
Distributed in the United Kingdom by GMC Distribution Services
Castle Place, 166 High Street, Lewes, East Sussex, England BN7 1XU
Distributed in Australia by Capricorn Link (Australia) Pty. Ltd.
P.O. Box 704, Windsor, NSW 2756, Australia

Manufactured in the United States of America
All Rights Reserved

Sterling ISBN-13: 978-0-8069-8832-0 Hardcover
        ISBN-10: 0-8069-8832-0
        ISBN-13: 978-1-4027-4405-1 Paperback
        ISBN-10: 1-4027-4405-6

For information about customs editions, special sales, or premium and corporate purchases, please contact the Sterling Special Sales Department at 800-805-5489 or specialsales@sterlingpub.com

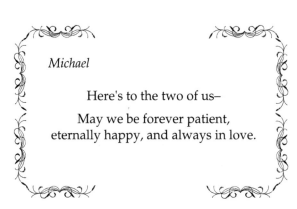

Michael

Here's to the two of us–

May we be forever patient,
eternally happy, and always in love.

Table of

Contents

Introduction

The custom of drinking a "toast" to the prosperity, happiness, luck, or good health of another dates back to antiquity.

It is impossible to point to the moment when the first crude vessel was raised in honor of an ancient god, but what we do know is that the custom of drinking to health permeated the ancient world and that over time the simple act of toasting another became embellished and intertwined with other customs. At some point along the way, toasts were created to celebrate success, happiness, and all other emotions or events worth honoring. Some time after the seventeenth century, the gesture of clinking glasses became popular. One legendary explanation for such glass clinking is that all five senses should come into play to get the greatest pleasure from a drink. It is tasted, touched, seen, smelled, and—with the clink—heard.

✄ Best Wishes ✑

May you have enough happiness to keep
you sweet; enough trials to keep you strong;
enough sorrow to keep you human; enough
hope to keep you happy; enough failure to keep
you humble; enough success to keep you eager;
enough friends to give you comfort; enough
faith and courage in yourself to banish
depression; enough wealth to meet your needs;
enough determination to make each day a
better day than yesterday.

May there always be work for
your hands to do.
May your purse always hold a coin or two.
May the sun always shine
on your windowpane.
May a rainbow be certain
to follow each rain.
May the hand of a friend
always be near to you.
May God fill your heart
with gladness to cheer you.

Irish

May you look back on the past with as much
pleasure as you look forward to the future.

Irish

✎ Courage ✍

Dr. Charles Garfield, author of *Peak Performance*, tells a humorous story about differentiating between courage and fear.

A very wealthy man, he notes, bought a huge ranch in Arizona and invited some of his close associates in to see it. After touring some of the 1,500 acres of mountains, rivers and grasslands, he took everyone back to the house, which was as spectacular as the scenery. Behind the exquisite home was the largest swimming pool in all of Arizona. There was just one thing about it, however, that was unusual. The gigantic swimming pool was filled with alligators.

The rich owner explained that he valued courage more than any other character trait. Courage, he claimed, was what made him a billionaire. "In fact, courage is such a powerful virtue that if anyone is courageous enough to jump in that pool, swim through those alligators and make it to the other side, I'll give them anything they want. Anything–my house, my land, my money."

Of course, everyone laughed at the absurd challenge and proceeded to follow the owner into the house for lunch. Suddenly, they heard a splash. Turning around they saw a young man swimming for his life across the pool. He was thrashing at the water as the alligators swarmed after him.

After death-defying seconds, the young man made it, unharmed, to the other side. The rich host and his guests applauded his efforts. And the billionaire stuck to his promise. He said to the dripping wet fellow, "You are indeed a man of courage and I will stick to my word. What do you want? You can have anything, my house, my land, my money—just tell me what you want and it is yours."

The young swimmer breathed heavily for a few moments, looked up at the host and said, "I want to know just one thing. Who the hell pushed me into that pool?"

To the two of you who are awaiting marriage, I applaud your courage and understand your fear as you wait on the edge of the pool to jump or be nudged...into matrimony.

Discretion

With some folks,
it's what you don't say that counts.

It is the little rift within the lute
that by and by may make
the music mute!

Alfred Lord Tennyson

I have never been hurt
by anything I did not say.

Calvin Coolidge

To keep your marriage brimming,
With love in the loving cup,
Whenever you're wrong, admit it;
Whenever you're right, shut up!

Ogden Nash

Dreams

I avoid looking forward or backward, and try to keep looking upward.   *Charlotte Brontë*

The greatest achievement was, at first and for a time, a dream. The oak sleeps in the acorn; the bird waits in the egg; and in the highest vision of the soul, a waking angel stirs. Dreams are the seedlings of realities.   *James Allen*

Go confidently in the direction of your dreams! Live the life you've imagined! As you simplify your life, the laws of the universe will be simpler; solitude will not be solitude, poverty will not be poverty, nor weakness weakness.
                                        Henry David Thoreau

Come live with me, and be my love,
And we will some new pleasures prove
Of golden sands, and crystal brooks,
With silken lines, and silver hooks.

                                        John Donne

There are two worlds: the world that we can measure with line and rule, and the world that we feel with our hearts and imagination.

Leigh Hunt

We grow great by dreams. All big men are dreamers. They see things in the soft haze of a spring day or the red fire of a long winter's evening. Some of us let these great dreams die, but others nourish and protect them; nurse them through bad days till they bring them to the sunshine and light which comes always to those who sincerely hope that their dreams will come true.

Woodrow Wilson

Friendship

Silences make the real conversations between friends.

Not the saying but the never needing to say is what counts.

Friendship makes a fair day out of the storms and tempests of affections and brings daylight to the darkness and confusion of thoughts.

Mme. de Lafayette

Friendship is the wine of life!   *Edward Young*

Friendship is always a sweet responsibility, never an opportunity.   *Kahlil Gibran*

Friendship improves happiness, and abates misery, by doubling our joy, and dividing our grief.   *Joseph Addison*

The most I can do for my friend is simply be his friend.   *Henry David Thoreau*

Friendship is love with understanding.

Ancient Proverb

A real friend is one who walks in when the rest of the world walks out.   *Walter Winchell*

Friendship is a union of spirits, a marriage of hearts, and the bond of virtue.   *William Penn*

Friendship is a sheltering tree.
Samuel Taylor Coleridge

A constant friend
is a thing rare
and hard to find.

Plutarch

Thou wert my guide, philosopher and friend.
Alexander Pope

Promises may get friends, but it is performance that must nurse and keep them.
Owen Felltham

A true friend is the greatest of all blessings.
Duc de la Rochefoucauld

There is no possession more valuable than a good and faithful friend.   *Socrates*

What is a friend: A single soul dwelling in two bodies.
Aristotle

May the road rise to meet you.
May the wind be always at your back,
the sun shine warm upon your face,
and the rain fall soft upon your fields,
and, until we meet again, may
God hold you in the hollow of His hand.
Irish

We have been friends together in sunshine and shade.
Caroline Norton

There is no possession more valuable than a good and faithful friend.
Socrates

Friendship is the marriage of the soul.
Voltaire

Without a friend, the world is but
a wilderness. A man may have a thousand
intimate acquaintances and not a friend
among them all. If you have one
true friend, think yourself rich.

May our house
always be too small
to hold all of our friends.

Myrtle Reed

The ornaments of your house
will be the guests who frequent it.

To my friend–

I love you not only for what you are,
but for what I am when I am with you.
I love you not only for what you have
made of yourself,
but for what you are making of me.
I love you because you have done
more than any creed could have done
to make me good,
and more than any fate could have done to
make me happy.
You have done it without a touch, without
a word, without a sign.
You have done it by being yourself.
Perhaps that is what being a friend means,
after all.

From the Heart

Remember to always make the little decisions with your head and the big decisions with your heart.

I always see better with my heart.

As a man thinketh in his heart, so is he.

Proverbs 23:7

Fair is the white star of twilight,
And the sky clearer
At the day's end;
But she is fairer,
and she is dearer,
She, my heart's friend.

Fair is the white star
of twilight,
And the moon roving
To the sky's end;
But she is fairer,
Better worth loving,
She, my heart's friend.

Shoshone Love Song

See, I will not forget you.
I have written your name on my heart.
Jo Packham

I would wrap you in white linen and
lilacs....and deliver you to a morning in May.
Michael Macfarlane

When the heart is right, "for" and
"against" are forgotten.

The heart is wiser than the intellect.
Josiah G. Holland

For where the heart is, that is sure to be where
your treasure is.   *Matthew 6:21*

Better is a heart full of love, than a mind filled
with knowledge.   *Charles Dickens*

For lovers who keep on keeping on
with their love there is never an end to the
glories of marriage.

∽ Joy & Happiness ∾

The supreme happiness of life is the
conviction of being loved for yourself, or more
correctly, being loved in spite of yourself.

Victor Hugo

Joy is not in things:
It is in us.

Wagner

Remember this...that very little is needed
to make a happy life.

Marcus Aurelius

Never forget that those who bring
happiness to the lives of others
cannot keep it from themselves.

Maurice Maeterlinck

The time to be happy is now;
the place to be happy is here.

Robert G. Ingersoll

Happiness is something to accompany our living, striving, and pursuing, not to follow it. We must look for happiness along the road... not at the end of it. Cheerfulness must be made a constant daily habit. There is a tremendous amount of satisfaction to be gotten out of the hardest journeys through life.

Alfred A. Montapert

Happiness sneaks in through a door you didn't know you left open.

John Barrymore

People spend their lives in anticipation of being extremely happy in the future.
But all we own is the PRESENT...NOW.
PAST opportunities are gone.
FUTURE opportunities may, or may not, come.
NOW is all we have.
We must enjoy each day–one at a time.
We are here on a short visit.
Be sure to smell the flowers.

Alfred A. Montapert

Happiness seems made to be shared.

Jean Racine

To get the full value of joy you must have someone to divide it with. *Mark Twain*

Happiness is like a kiss–it feels best when you give it to someone else.

He is a wise man who does not grieve for the things which he has not, but rejoices for those which he has. *Epictetus*

Happy is the man who has broken the chains which hurt the mind, and has given up worrying once and for all. *Ovid*

If you depend on another to make you happy, you will be endlessly disappointed.

The grand essentials to happiness in this life are something to do, someone to love, and something to hope for. *Joseph Addison*

Weeping may endure for a night, but joy cometh in the morning. *Psalms 30:5*

If it is to be, it is up to me.

He that thinks himself the happiest man
really is so.   *C. C. Colton*

The way to Happiness:
Keep your heart free from hate,
Your mind from worry.
Live simply. Expect little. Give much.

Happiness resides not in
possessions and not in gold;
the feeling of happiness
dwells in the soul.

Democritus

Happiness is an inside job.
Father of H. Jackson Brown, Jr.

To repress a harsh answer, to confess a fault,
and to stop (right or wrong) in the midst of
self-defense in gentle submission sometimes
requires a struggle like life and death.
But these three efforts are the golden threads
with which domestic happiness is woven.
Caroline Gilaman

23

Happiness is not a state to arrive at, but a
manner of traveling.   *Margaret Lee Runbeck*

To love is to place our happiness in the
happiness of another.   *G.W. von Leibniz*

A program for happiness–

> To live content with small means;
> To seek elegance rather than luxury,
> and refinement rather than fashion;
> To be worthy, not respectable,
> and wealthy, not rich;
> To study hard, think quietly,
> talk gently, act frankly;
> To listen to the stars and birds,
> to babes and sages with open heart;
> To bear all cheerfully, and bravely,
> await occasions, hurry never;
> In a word, to let the spiritual, unbidden and
> unconscious, grow up through the common.
>
> *William Henry Chandler*

Happiness is good health and a bad memory.
     Ingrid Bergman

Love is all you need.   *Lennon/McCartney*

Be happy. It is one way of being wise.

Colette

Remember always: Arrows pierce the body,
but harsh words pierce the soul.

Spanish Proverb

There is only one person in the world who can
really make you happy...and YOU are that
person. Happiness is a do-it-yourself job.

Alfred A. Montapert

Each day make it a challenge to do your best...
live your best... For today will soon be
tomorrow, and tomorrow will soon be forever.

The Way to Happiness

Music washes away from the soul, the dust of
everyday life.

Berthold Auerbach

Love cometh like sunshine after rain.

William Shakespeare

Kindness

A tiny bouquet of fresh-cut flowers,
Can fill a room with sunshine.
A little act of kindness
Can fill a heart with joy.

Katherine Nelson

I would like to have engraved inside every
wedding band, "Be kind to one another."
This is the Golden Rule of marriage and the
secret of making love last through the years.

Randolph Ray

Be ye kind to one another.　　*Ephesians 4:32*

How often a careless, unkind word
spoken can spoil your day, wreck some
big job or deal, hurt a loved one, lose a friend.
Many of us, through ignorance,
thoughtlessness, or want of judgment,
wound those whom we love best and
most wish to help.

Alfred A. Montapert

Always be kinder than necessary.

James M. Barrie

A hug is worth a thousand words.

It is a little embarrassing that after
forty-five years of research and study,
the best advice I can give to people is to be
a little kinder to each other.

Aldous Huxley

 ⤶   **Love**   ⤷

Our love is the greatest
gift we can give one another.

There are as many kinds of love
as many kinds of light,
And every kind of love
makes a glory in the night.
There is love that stirs the heart,
and love that gives it rest,
But the love that leads life upwards
is the noblest and the best.

Henry Van Dyke

Every house where love abides
And friendship is a guest,
Is surely home, and home sweet home
For there the heart can rest.　　*Henry Van Dyke*

A bell is not a bell until you ring it.
A song is not a song until you sing it.
Love in your heart is not put there to stay.
Love is not yours–till you give it away.

Oscar Hammerstein

The most precious possession that ever comes
to a man in this world is a woman's heart.

Josiah Gilbert Holland

Since we shall love each other,
I shall be great
And you rich.

Victor Hugo

Only in love are unity and
duality not in conflict.   *Rabindranath Tagore*

A coward is incapable of exhibiting love;
it is the prerogative of the brave.

Mahatma Ghandi

When love is concerned,
too much is not ever enough.

Pierre-Augustin Caron de Beaumarchais

O my Luve's like a red, red rose
That's newly sprung in June:
O my Luve's like the melodie
That's sweetly played in tune.
As fair art thou, my bonnie lass,
So deep in luve am I;
And I will luve thee still, my dear,
Till a' the seas gang dry

Robert Burns

Wise are they, who sense that the surest
way to be fully loved is to love fully.

...The secret of Health, Happiness and Long
Life: If you simply learn how to accept and
express love, you will live longer...be
happier...grow healthier. For love is a
powerful force. *Alfred A. Montapert*

Him that I love, I wish to be free—
even from me. *Anne Morrow Lindbergh*

Love is to life what sunshine
is to plants and flowers.
Tom Blandi

To love is to admire with the heart;
and to admire is to love with the mind.

T. Gautier

Love is like a rose, the joy of all the earth...

Christina Rossetti

It was not in the winter,
Our loving was cast!
It was the time of roses,
We plucked them as we passed!

Thomas Hood

The supreme happiness of life is the
conviction that we are loved.   *Victor Hugo*

Here's a health to the future;
A sigh for the past;
We can love and remember;
and hope to the last,
And for all the base lies
That the almanacs hold
While there's love in the heart,
We can never grow old.

Love is not a matter of counting the years;
it is making the years count.   *William Smith*

There is an old story which supposedly comes from Vermont. They say this old grouch lived with his wife for twenty-one years and never spoke one single word. Then one morning at breakfast he broke the silence with, "Darling, sometimes when I think how much you mean to me it is almost more than I can do to keep from telling you!"

Charlie W. Shedd

If I could wrap love
in a shiny silver box
with a big blue ribbon...
it would be my gift to you.

Any time that is not spent on love is wasted.

Tasso

When Silence speaks for Love,
she has much to say.   *Richard Garnett*

One of the attributes of love, like art, is to bring harmony and order out of chaos.

Molly Haskell

"Love does not rejoice at wrong, but rejoices in the right."   *I Corinthians 13:6*

"Love is what you go through together"
Thornton Wilder

Written by a ten year old named Tommy
for his school composition: What is love? Love
is something that makes two people think they
are pretty even when nobody else does. It also
makes them sit close together on a bench even
when there's plenty of room. It's something
which makes two people very quiet when you
are around. And when they think you're gone
they talk about roses and dreams.
And that's all I know about love
until I grow up.
Charlie W. Shedd

French saying: I love you more than yesterday,
less than tomorrow.

There's one sad truth in life I've found
While journeying east to west.
The only folks we really wound
Are those we love the best.
We flatter those we scarcely know,
We please the fleeting guest.
And deal full many a thoughtless blow,
To those we love the best.

"What is REAL?" asked the Rabbit one day, when they were lying side by side near the nursery fender, before Nana came to tidy the room. "Does it mean having things that buzz inside you and a stick-out handle?"

"Real isn't how you are made," said the Skin Horse. "It's a thing that happens to you. When a child loves you for a long, long time, not just to play with, but REALLY loves you, then you become Real."

"Does it hurt?" asked the Rabbit.

"Sometimes," said the Skin Horse, for he was always truthful. "When you are Real you don't mind being hurt."

"Does it happen all at once, like being wound up," he asked, "or bit by bit?"

"It doesn't happen all at once ," said the Skin Horse. "You become. It takes a long time. That's why it doesn't often happen to people who break easily, or have sharp edges, or who have to be carefully kept. Generally, by the time you are Real, most of your hair has been loved off, and your eyes drop out and you get loose in the joints and very shabby. But these things don't matter at all, because once you are Real, you can't be ugly except to people who don't understand."

The Velveteen Rabbit
Margery Williams

May we always love each other...
as we are, not as we were.   *Michael Macfarlane*

There is no surprise more magical than the
surprise of being loved. It is God's finger
on man's shoulder.   *Charles Morgan*

There is nothing greater in life than loving
another, and being loved in return.

Love must be set free, and only when it comes
back to us will we know the real thing.

May our love be perfect, even if we are not.
    Michael Macfarlane

Love is the master key that opens the gates of
happiness.   *Oliver Wendell Holmes*

Love doesn't sit there like a stone, it has
to be made, like bread; remade all of
the time, made new.   *Ursula K. LeGuin*

Love at first sight is easy to understand; it is when two people have been looking at each other for a lifetime that it becomes a miracle.

Sam Levenson

Love needs no words.
Love makes a heart smile.
Love is all there is.

The more you love each other, the closer you will come to God.

Love is like war, easy to begin but very hard to stop.   *The Toastmaster's Treasure Chest*

Men always want to be a woman's first love; women have a more subtle instinct: what they like is to be a man's last romance.

To be in love is merely to be in a state of perpetual anesthesia.

The Toastmaster's Treasure Chest

Love: two minds without a single thought.

Phillip Barry

Love is woman's eternal spring and man's eternal fall. *The Toastmaster's Treasure Chest*

Our love is like the misty rain that falls softly– but floods the river. *African Proverb*

Love comforteth like sunshine after rain. *William Shakespeare*

Your love is comfort in sadness, quietness in tumult, rest in weariness, hope in despair. *Marion C. Garretty*

Treasure the love you receive above all. It will survive long after your gold and good health have vanished. *Og Mandino*

Love is the triumph of imagination over intelligence. *The Toastmaster's Treasure Chest*

No one acts more foolishly than a wise man in love. *The Toastmaster's Treasure Chest*

You can see them alongside the shuffle-board courts in Florida or on the porches of the old folks' homes up north: an old man with snow-white hair, a little hard of hearing, reading the newspaper through a magnifying glass; an old woman in a shapeless dress, her knuckles gnarled by arthritis, wearing sandals to ease her aching arches. They are holding hands...They are in love, they have always been in love, although sometimes they would have denied it. And because they have been in love they have survived everything that life could throw at them, even their own failures.

Ernest Havemann

I learned the real meaning of love. Love is absolute loyalty. People fade, looks fade, but loyalty never fades. You can depend so much on certain people, you can set your watch by them. And that's love, even if it doesn't seem very exciting.

Sylvester Stallone

Everybody has to be somebody to somebody to be anybody.

Malcolm S. Forbes

Love must be learned, and learned again and again; there is no end to it.

Katherine Anne Porter

Love is the state in which man sees things most decidedly as they are not.

The Toastmaster's Treasure Chest

Remember that if you care,
it will always show.

I would be friends with you
and have your love.

William Shakespeare

Those who love deeply never grow old; they may die of old age, but they die young.

Sir Arthur Wing Pinero

Sensual pleasure passes and vanishes in the twinkling of an eye, but the friendship between us, the mutual confidence, the delights of the heart, the enchantment of the soul, these things do not perish and can never be destroyed. I shall love you until I die.

Voltaire to Mme. Denis

Love is nothing without friendship.

If you would be loved, love and be lovable.
Benjamin Franklin

Love is best.   *Robert Browning*

Love demands infinitely less than friendship.
George Jean Nathan

To love a person means to agree to grow old
with him.   *Albert Camus*

Mediocre passions are eloquent. Only great
ones are silent.   *Christine de Suede*

Love strikes like lightning and leaves its
indelible traces forever on the heart.

Love is love's reward.
John Dryd

Love understands and therefore waits.

That love which is born so quickly, those irresistible impulses, are like certain hothouse plants, whose artificial and spontaneous blooming is no doubt faster, but only lasts a moment; whereas real love that grows with patience, according to the laws of nature, is like the offspring of the oak; it grows unaided and slowly; it looks pail and bare for a long time, but it holds in its roots a whole century of future.   *Mme. Emile de Girardin*

The sweetest love is unconditional.

Love is patient and kind; love is not jealous or boastful; it is not arrogant or rude. Love does not insist on its own way; it is not irritable or resentful; it does not rejoice at wrong, but rejoices in the right. Love bears all things, believes all things, hopes all things, endures all things.

Love never ends;...So faith, hope, love abide, these three; but the greatest of these is love.
                    I Corinthians 13:4–8, 13

Women love with all their heart and men love with all their strength.

Comtesse de Beauharnais

Hell is a place where there is no love. If Satan could love, he would cease to be evil.

Saint Therese

I Love You–

I love you for what you are, but I love you yet more for what you are going to be.

I love you not so much for your realities as for your ideals. I pray for your desires that they may be great, rather than for your satisfactions, which may be so hazardously little.

A satisfied flower is one whose petals are about to fall. The most beautiful rose is one hardly more than a bud wherein the pangs and ecstasies of desire are working for larger and finer growth.

Not always shall you be what you are now.

You are going forward toward something great. I am on the way with you and therefore I love you.   *Carl Sandburg*

Love is only for the young,
the middle-aged, and the old.

A Syrian Legend

Three men stood, one stormy night, at the threshold of a wayside cottage. Their knock at the door was answered by a child who asked their names and the purpose of their visit.

One of the two spoke saying: "My name is Love. My companions are Luck and Riches. We are seeking places for rest and refreshment. One of us would be pleased to receive the hospitality of this home tonight, and the choice of who it is to be we leave with you." The girl was bewildered; she ran and called the other members of the family, who gathered quickly to decide which of the three distinguished callers they would receive.

They repeated over and over again the names of their three would-be guests, studied their characters, and listened again to the request that was made.

Wisdom ruled the family's decision, and the choice was soon made. In unison they exclaimed: "We will entertain Love!"

But the family was perplexed to find that Luck and Riches accompanied the invited Love to the preferred room. Observing their

astonishment, Love turned to the kind hosts
and said, with a divine smile: "Be not alarmed.
Wherever I am made welcome, there my
companions also will make their home."

And that home, so say the Syrians whose
legend this is, was blessed forever more.

I never thought I could really love anything
without four wheels and a stick shift.

Michael Macfarlane

Being loved by you makes me feel protected
but not smothered, challenged but not
threatened, directed but not controlled, wanted
but not possessed. You are the one with whom I
am not afraid to become "we."

Your words dispel all of the care in the world
and make me happy....They are as necessary to
me now as sunlight and air....Your words are
my food, your breath my wine–you are
everything to me.

Sarah Bernhardt

You hold most fast to the people you love
by gently letting them go.

Love may not make the world go around,
but it sure makes the trip worthwhile!

Eric Johnson

True love has no maximum. For those who
keep opening new roads into each other's hearts
each day and very often, new possibilities are
forever opening up and the greatest love goes
on to new greatness. *Charlie W. Shedd*

Modern fiction, says one critic, runs too much
to love. Yes, and modern love runs too much to
fiction. *Wall Street Journal*

What do I get from loving you? Loving you.

John-Roger

We never live so intensely as when we love
strongly. *Walter Rauschenbusch*

Love is a portion of the soul itself, and it is of
the same nature as the celestial breathing of the
atmosphere of paradise. *Victor Hugo*

Love is the greatest educational institution
on earth.   *Channing Pollock*

The love we have in our youth is superficial
compared to the love that an old man has for
his old wife.   *Will Durant*

Love is the true means by which the world is
enjoyed.   *Thomas Traherne*

When one has only fully entered the realm of
love, the world–no matter how imperfect –
becomes rich and beautiful and consists solely
of opportunity...   *Soren Kierkegaard*

In love, all of life's contradictions dissolve and
disappear.   *Rabindranath Tagore*

Love is friendship set on fire.   *Jeremy Taylor*

The course of true love never did run smooth.
                              William Shakespeare

Love the things you love for what they are.

The measure of one's devotion is doing,
not merely saying. Love is demonstration,
not merely declaration.

How do I love thee? Let me count the ways....
Elizabeth Barrett Browning

We are shaped and fashioned by what we
love.   *Goethe*

Love gives naught but itself and takes naught
but from itself. Love possesses not nor would
it be possessed; for love is sufficient unto love.
Kahlil Gibran

Once you have learned to love, you have
learned to live.   *Walter M. Germain*

Love is a taste of paradise.

Love is the heart's immortal thirst to be
completely known and all forgiven.
Henry Van Dyke

Love is the fusion of two hearts–
the union of two lives–
the coming together of two tributaries.

Peter Marshall

Love gives us in a moment what we can hardly
attain by effort after years of toil.   *Goethe*

Among those whom I like, I can find no
common denominator, but among those whom
I love, I can: all of them make me laugh!

W.H. Auden

A wise lover values not so much the gift
of the lover as the love of the giver.

Thomas á Kempis

Love is not a union merely between two
creatures–it is a union between two spirits.

Frederick W. Robertson

To love someone
is to see a miracle
invisible to others.

Francois Mauriac

There is only one terminal dignity–love.
And the story of a love is not important–
what is important is that one is
capable of love. It is perhaps the
only glimpse we are permitted
of eternity.

Helen Hays

Love is the only sane and satisfactory answer to
the problem of human existence.

Eric Fromm

Love is an act of endless forgiveness,
a tender look which becomes a habit.

Peter Ustinov

Here's to the love that I hold for thee;
May it day by day grow stronger.
May it last as long as your love for me,
And not one second longer!

Because I love you truly,
Because you love me, too,
My very greatest happiness
Is sharing life with you.

Brew me a cup for a winter's night.
For the wind howls loud and the furies fight;
Spice it with love and stir it with care,
And I'll toast your bright eyes,
my sweetheart fair.

Minna Thomas Antrim

Come in the evening,
or come in the morning,
Come when you are looked for,
or come without warning,
A thousand welcomes you will
find here before you,
And the oftener you come here
the more I'll adore you.

Irish

The love you give away is the only love
you keep. *Elbert Hubbard*

I would be friends with you
and have your love.

Man

It's a funny thing that when a man hasn't got anything on earth to worry about, he goes off and gets married.   *Robert Frost*

This fate is the newly married sir's.
To think she's his and find he's hers.
                    S. H. Dewhurst

Before marriage, a man will lie awake all night thinking about something you said; after marriage, he'll fall asleep before you finish saying it.   *Helen Rowland*

A great man is he who has not lost the heart of a child.   *Mencius*

A toast to the groom–and discretion to his bachelor friends.

The young man who wants to marry happily should pick out a good mother and marry one of her daughters...any one will do.
                    J. Ogden Armour

Drink, my buddies, drink with discerning;
Wedlock's a lane where there is no turning;
Never was owl more blind than lover;
Drink and be merry, lads; and think it over.

Bachelor party toast

Here's to the freedom and pleasures of the
single life...May my memory now fail me!

Michael Macfarlane

Tenderness and kindness are not signs of
weakness and despair, but manifestations of
strength and resolution.   *Kahlil Gibran*

From the bride–

> To the men I've loved
> To the men I've kissed
> My heartfelt apologies
> To the men I've missed!

Here's to man–he is like a coal oil lamp; he is
not especially bright; he is often turned down;
he generally smokes; and he frequently goes out
at night.

❧ Marriage ❧

What is thine is mine, and all mine is thine.
Plautus

Never, never, never, never give up.
Winston Churchill

Remember that the big problems
always start out small.

You will learn that the best way to appreciate
something is to go without it for a while.

Marriage is like a blind date. Sometimes you
just have to have a little faith.

It is the man and woman united that makes
the complete human being. Separate she lacks
his force of body and strength of reason; he her
softness, sensibility and acute discernment.
Together they are most likely to succeed
in the world. *Benjamin Franklin*

Remember that if you ever put your
marital problems on the back burner they
are sure to boil over.

Marriage is a mistake
every man should make.
George Jessel

By all means marry; if you get a good wife,
you'll become happy; if you get a bad one,
you'll become a philosopher.   *Socrates*

A happy marriage is still the greatest treasure
within the gift of fortune.   *Eden Phillpotts*

Marriage is our last, best chance to grow up.
Joseph Barth

My most brilliant achievement was my ability
to be able to persuade my wife to marry me.
Winston Churchill

I will tell you the real secret of how to stay married. Keep the cave clean. They want the cave clean and spotless. Air-conditioned, if possible. Sharpen his spear, and stick it in his hand when he goes out in the morning to spear that bear; and when the bear chases him, console him when he comes home at night, and tell him what a big man he is, and then hide the spear so he doesn't fall over it and stab himself...

Jerome Chodorov and Joseph Fields

God, the best maker of all marriages,
Combine your hearts in one.

William Shakespeare

Marriage is the alliance of two people, one of whom never remembers birthdays and the other who never forgets. *Ogden Nash*

Happy marriages begin when we marry the one we love, and they blossom when we love the one we married. *Sam Levenson*

People with ungovernable tempers should never marry; people who can't accept reality should never marry; people who don't enjoy responsibility should never marry. In fact, an awful lot of people should never marry.

Olivia de Havilland

There is a fantasy that you fall in love, get married and everything will automatically be all right. But in reality, falling in love is like a vacation on a Caribbean island. Marriage, on the other hand, is like scratching a living from the steep, stony slopes of Sicily. They are two separate events.

David Birney

Marriage is a meal where the soup is better than the dessert.

Austin O'Malley

As told to a new bride by her father: "Your marriage will be perfect when the rocks in your husband's head fill the holes in yours."

The best way to hold a man is in your arms.

Mae West

A perfect marriage could only happen between a blind wife and a deaf husband.

There is a three step strategy to surviving married life if all else fails.

Step 1: Go to the store and buy enough marbles to fill a glass jar and put the jar filled with marbles somewhere easy to see.

Step 2: Every time your husband (or wife) does something to upset or annoy you, go to the jar, get a marble, and throw it out the window.

Step 3: Follow this sequence until all of the marbles are gone.

> *Theory:* Once you have lost all of your marbles, your husband (or wife) won't bother you any more.

Can You Afford Marriage?

The bride, white of hair, stoops over her cane,
Her footsteps, uncertain, need guiding,
While down the church aisle,
with a wan, toothless smile,
The groom in a wheelchair comes riding.
And who is this elderly couple thus wed?
You'll find when you closely explore it,
That here is the rare, most conservative pair,
Who waited till they could afford it!

Albert Einstein was asked on his 50th wedding anniversary, "To what do you attribute the success of your marriage?" Professor Einstein offered this profound response: "When we first got married, we made a pact. It was this: In our life together, it was decided I would make all of the big decisions and my wife would make all of the little decisions. For fifty years, we have held true to that agreement. I believe that is the reason for the success in our marriage. However, the strange thing is that in fifty years, there hasn't been one big decision."

Marriage isn't a battle that someone is supposed to win.

Marriage is like life in this–that it is a field of battle, and not a bed of roses.

Robert Louis Stevenson

Seek a happy marriage with wholeness of heart, but do not expect to reach the promised land without going through some wilderness together. *Charlie W. Shedd*

Marriage is not just spiritual communion and passionate embraces; marriage is also three-meals-a-day and remembering to carry out the trash.   *Joyce Brothers*

Your success and happiness lie in you.
                                        Helen Keller

Memories of a 90-year-old grandmother of the three most important phrases her husband ever said to her, "I love you," "you are so beautiful," and "please forgive me."

Charlie Shedd's three most important words in any marriage: listen, listen, listen.

Two such as you with such a master speed
Cannot be parted nor be swept away
From one another once you are agreed
That life is only life forevermore
Together wing to wing and oar to oar.
                                        Robert Frost

Marriage is not so much finding the right person as it is being the right person.

Marriage may have turned into a junk bond. But nothing is so romantic as a risk.

Tracy Young

My wish for you is that you will marry someone who is so great that it will take a whole lifetime to know everything about him (her).

Charlie W. Shedd

On togetherness in marriage: It must include whatever amount of "apartness" is right for each of you. And if you allow plenty of room for the "apartness," this has a way of magnetizing the "togetherness."

Charlie W. Shedd

Don't hold on so tight that you squeeze one another away.

Marriage is not a ceremony! It is a creation!

Charlie W. Shedd

Marriage is three parts love and
seven parts forgiveness.
Langdon Mitchell

It is a lovely thing to have a husband and wife
developing together. That is what marriage
really means; helping one another to reach the
full status of being persons, responsible and
autonomous beings who do not run away
from life.   *Paul Tournier*

The sum which two married people owe to
one another defies calculation. It is an infinite
debt, which can only be discharged through all
eternity.   *Goethe*

There is no more lovely, friendly and
charming relationship, communion or company
than a good marriage.   *Martin Luther*

A successful marriage requires falling in love
many times, always with the same person.
Mignon McLaughlin

Marriage is that relation between
man and woman in which the
independence is equal, the dependence
mutual, and the obligation reciprocal.

Louis Kaufman Anspacher

Marriage is the greatest educational
institution on earth.

Channing Pollock

Marriage is a fan club with only two fans.

Adrian Henri

A marriage between mature people is not an
escape but a commitment shared by two people
that becomes part of their commitment to
themselves and society.   *Betty Friedan*

The key to a healthy marriage is to
keep your eyes wide open before you wed...
and half closed thereafter.

Don't look for a back door, before you go
through the front.

The great secret of a successful marriage is to treat all disasters as incidents and none of the incidents as disasters.

Harold Nicholson

Treasure the simplest of things. The grand events will come, and you will feel pride, but when you need comfort and direction, you will find it in the simple things.

Bernice Smith

Sometimes the hardest thing you will have to do is endure to the end of the day. Sometimes life will be so grand that the day will seem too short.

Bernice Smith

You will truly know you are married when the bills start to come and you learn to share the toothpaste.

Bernice Smith

If marriage is to be a success, one should obviously begin by marrying the right person.

Hermann Keyserling

Marriage: A community consisting of a
master, a mistress, and two slaves–making in
all, two.   *Ambrose Bierce*

Marriage is a wonderful institution,
but who wants to live in an institution?
                                                      Groucho Marx

A Second Marriage: To the triumph of hope
over experience.   *Samuel Johnson*

Passion

Marriage has many pains, but celibacy
has no pleasures.

May your fire never go out!

Today's the day,
Tonight's the night,
We've shot the stork–
So you're all right!

Past, Present & Future

Don't worry about the future,
The present is all thou hast,
The future will soon be the present,
And the present will soon be the past.

Every day should be passed as though
it were to be your last.

"You're lovely," he said on the
night they were wed.
"You're glowing," he said as
they bought the baby bed.
"You're tired," he said after everyone was fed.
"You're proud," he said as the
last one was wed.
"We made it," they said as they fell into bed.
On the carved stone it read,
"Together," they said.

Bernice Smith

Here's to the present–
and to hell with the past!
A health to the future and joy to the last!

ঔ Success ঙ

Success is dependent on effort.

Sophocles

He has achieved success who has lived well, laughed often and loved much.

Bessie Anderson Stanley

ঔ Troubles ঙ

Troubles are often the tools by which
God fashions us for better things.

Henry Ward Beecher

In the middle of difficulty lies opportunity.

Albert Einstein

If two people who love each other let a single moment come between them, it will grow and it will become a month, a year, a century until it becomes too late.   *Jean Giraudoux*

Wedding Toasts

Proceed with caution!

To the bridal couple–

May all of your troubles be little ones.

To the bridal couple from friends–

A health to you,
A wealth to you,
And the best that life can give to you.
May fortune still be kind to you.
And happiness be true to you,
And life be long and good to you,
Is the toast of all your friends to you.

To the bride from the groom–

Grow old with me!
The best is yet to be,
The last of life,
For which, the first is made.

Robert Browning

To the groom from a friend–

> To your good health, old friend,
> may you live for a thousand years,
> and I be there to count them.

Robert Smith Surtees

From the parents–

> It is written:
> "When children find true love,
> parents find true joy."
> Here's to your joy and ours,
> from this day forward.

It takes a woman twenty years to make a man
of her son, and another woman twenty minutes
to make a fool of him.   *Helen Rowland*

Nothing is worth more than this day.

Goethe

To mother–

> All that I am or hope to be,
> I owe to my angel mother.

Abraham Lincoln

A mother is a mother still,
The holiest thing alive.

Samuel Taylor Coleridge

No other worship abides and endures,
Faithful, unselfish, and patient, like yours.

Elizabeth Akers Allen

Blessed are the mothers, for they have
combined the practical and the spiritual into
one workable way of human life. They have
darned little stockings, mended little dresses,
washed little faces, and have pointed little eyes
to the stars and little souls to eternal things.

William L. Stidger

Oh, the love of a mother, love which none can
forget.

Victor Hugo

The love of a good mother for her children, is
in a class by itself. In other words, it is unique,
especially unique in fact. Unique because there
is nothing else like it in this big world in which
we all live and have our being. Especially
unique because it is ever-trustful, ever-devoted,
ever-forgiving, ever-tender, ever-unchanging,
and ever-enduring.

Samuel Johnson

Most all of the other beautiful things in life come by twos and threes, by dozens and hundreds. Plenty of roses, stars, sunsets, rainbows, brothers and sisters, aunts and cousins, but only one mother in the whole world.   *Kate Douglas Wiggin*

A mother is the truest friend we have. When trials, heavy and sudden fall upon us; when adversity takes the place of prosperity; when friends who rejoice with us in our sunshine desert us; when trouble thickens around us, still will she cling to us, and endeavor by her kind precepts and counsels to dissipate the clouds of darkness, and cause peace to return to our hearts.   *Washington Irving*

There are times when parenthood must seem like nothing more than feeding the mouth that bites you.   *Peter DeVries*

To father–
      Directly after God in heaven comes Papa.
                    Wolfgang Amadeus Mozart

When I was a boy of fourteen, my father was so ignorant I could hardly stand to have the old man around. But when I got to be twenty-one, I was astonished at how much he had learned in seven years.

Mark Twain

Dad, you couldn't have done it better. You are actually pretty amazing especially because I'm fully aware of the demanding brat I was.

John Travolta

My father told me the key to financial success was to have only one credit card.

Bruce Currie

My father has given me the greatest treasure a father can give– a piece of himself.

Suzanne Chazin

Dear Dad,
It is hard sometimes for a man to say this to another man; but I love you very much–always have, always will.

George Bush

There is a special bond between us. You
know–fathers just have a way of putting
everything together.   *Erika Cosby*

To the parents–

I think this is going to work. You can redecorate
my room!   *Michael Macfarlane*

To the bride and groom–
          There are only two lasting bequests
            we can hope to give our children.
          One of these is roots, the other wings.
                              Hodding Carter

        I have found the best way to give advice
          to my children is to find out what they
          want and then advise them to do it.
                              Harry S Truman

To the friends and family–

    A greeting to all of our friends and family;
        you are always welcome in our house.
            Please call before you come.
                          Michael Macfarlane

To the bride from her sister–

> May you always be as
> happy as you are today.
> May you always be as
> beautiful as you are today.
> May I have your white sweater?
>> *Michael Macfarlane*

> You don't choose your family.
> They are God's gift to you.
>> *Desmond Tutu*

> Health and happiness.

> Coming together is a beginning;
> keeping together is progress;
> working together is success.
>> *Henry Ford*

> May the two of you breakfast with Health,
> dine with Friendship, crack a bottle with Mirth,
> and sup with the goddess of Contentment.

> Always remember to forget the trouble that
> passes away, but never forget to remember the
> blessings that come each day.

To every lovely lady bright,
I wish a gallant faithful knight;
To every faithful lover, too,
I wish a trusting lady true.

Sir Walter Scott

Here's to the prettiest, here's to the wittiest,
Here's to the truest of all who are true,
Here's to the neatest one, here's to
the sweetest one,
Here's to them all in one–
Here's to you.

Here's to matrimony, the high sea for which no
compass has yet been invented.

Heinrich Heine

Never go to bed mad. Stay up and fight.

Phyllis Diller

Nothing is worth more than this day.

Goethe

Here's to you who halves my sorrows
and doubles my joys.

There is no scientific answer for success.
You can't define it. You've simply got to
live it and do it.

Anita Roddick

If you want to sacrifice the
admiration of many men for the
criticism of one,
go ahead, get married.

Katharine Hepburn

Here's to Dan Cupid, the little squirt,
He's lost his pants, he's lost his shirt,
He's lost most everything but his aim,
Which shows that love is a losing game!

Here's to the wings of love–
May they never molt a feather;
Till my big boots and your little shoes
Are under the bed together!

Here's to the woman that I love,
And here's to the woman that loves me,
And here's to all those that love her that I love,
And to those that love her that love me.

74

To be happy with a man you must understand
him a lot and love him a little.
To be happy with a woman you must love
her a lot and not try to understand her at all.
Helen Rowland

See as a child sees;
the joy, the wonder, the hope.

I have known many, liked a few,
loved one–here's to you!

A toast to love and laughter and
happily ever after.

Something great and wonderful is happening
today, and I am part of it.　　*Dr. Robert Scott*

Down the hatch, to a striking match!

May your dreams ride on the wings of angels
who know their way home to the skies.

I wish you all things good and wonderful.

Here's to *my* mother-in-law's daughter,
Here's to *her* father-in-law's son;
And here's to the vows we've just taken,
And the life we've just begun.
Here's to the bride that is to be,
Here's to the groom she'll wed,
May all their troubles be light as bubbles
Or the feathers that make up their bed!
Here's to the groom with bride so fair,
and here's to the bride with groom so rare!
Here's to the husband and here's to the wife;
May they remain lovers for life.

May the special moments of today be the most
remembered memories of tomorrow.

With trumpets and fanfare,
I wish you the happiest of all days.

May your eyes stay filled with stars and your
heart with visions of dreams yet to come.

May you always share your love
and laughter.

I wish you the time to celebrate
the simple joys.

The man or woman you really love will never grow old to you. Through the wrinkles of time, through the bowed frame of years, you will always see the dear face and feel the warm heart union of your eternal love.

Alfred A. Montapert

Don't walk in front of me,
I may not follow.
Don't walk behind me,
I may not lead;
Walk beside me,
And just be my friend.

Irish

Let us celebrate this occasion with wine and sweet words. *Latin Proverb*

Never above you. Never below you. Always beside you. *Walter Winchell*

The world is gay and colorful,
And life itself is new.
And I am very grateful for
The Friend I found in you.

ᓚ Woman ᓂ

Once a woman decides she wants something,
never underestimate her ability to get it.

Sometimes you have to kiss a lot of frogs
before you find a prince.

Every woman has two husbands: the one she is
given, and the one she creates.

More marriages are ruined nowadays by the
common sense of the husband than by anything
else. How can a woman be expected to be
happy with a man who insists on treating her as
if she were a perfectly rational being?

Oscar Wilde

A woman is a miracle of divine contradictions.

Jules Michelet

Love is the only game not called
on a count of darkness.

May you always be happy,
And live at your ease;
Get a kind husband
And do as you please.

J. S. Ogilvie

A woman should never accept a lover without the consent of her heart, nor a husband without the consent of her judgment.

Ninon de Lenclos

What is it that love does to women? Without it, she only sleeps; with it alone, she lives.

Ouida

Women are too imaginative and sensitive to have much logic. *Mme. du Deffand*

A woman's head is always influenced by her heart, but a man's heart is always influenced by his head. *Countess of Blessington*

By the time you swear you're his,
shivering and sighing;
and he vows his passion is infinite, undying—
Lady, make a note of this: One of you is lying!

The Toastmaster's Treasure Chest

The perfect mate, despite what *Cosmopolitan* says, does not exist, no matter how many of those tests you take.

Suzanne Britt Jordan

When a woman is in love, there is something about her that betrays her feelings in spite of herself. No matter how well she guards her secret, it will spill out of her heart as from an overflowing cup. She will try in vain to hide the radiance of that inward light shinning from her eyes, her lips and all of her features.

Princess Olga Cantacuzene

Women and elephants never forget!

Dorothy Parker

I do not believe women ever get sensible, not even through prolonged association with their husbands.

Dorothy L. Sayers

Don't compromise yourself.
You are all you've got.

Betty Ford

Love, an episode in the life of man, is the entire story of the life of a woman.

Mme. de Staël

A woman will always cherish the memory of the man who wanted to marry her; a man of the woman who didn't.   *Viola Brothers Shore*

A woman must have money
and a room of her own.

Virginia Woolf

Women are the glue that holds our day-to-day world together.   *Anna Quindlen*

Nobody wants to kiss when they are hungry.

Attributed to Dorothy Dix

Women love always: when earth slips from them, they take refuge in heaven.

George Sand

A wise woman puts a grain of sugar into everything she says to a man, and takes a grain of salt with everything he says to her.

Helen Rowland

Be bold in what you stand for and careful what you fall for.
Ruth Boorstin

A liberated woman is one who has sex before marriage and a job after.
Gloria Steinem

It is a waste of time trying to change a man's character. You have to accept your husband as he is.
Queen Elizabeth II

Don't accept rides from strange men–and remember that all men are as strange as hell.
Robin Morgan

Words to the Wise

Some say it is holding on that makes you strong. Some say it is the letting go.

What we anticipate seldom occurs; but what we least expect generally happens.

Benjamin Disraeli

Those who never risk
will never lose.
But neither will they grow.
Those who never feel
will never cry.
But neither will they laugh.
Those who never love
will never hurt.
But neither will they live.

When in doubt, tell the truth.
Mark Twain

Most people are about as happy as they make
up their minds to be.   *Abraham Lincoln*

There is probably but one answer to the
question, "What do we get out of life?" And
that is, we get out of life exactly what we put
into it, but we get that back in great abundance.
William Ross

Having it all doesn't necessarily mean having it
all at once.   *Stephanie Luethkehans*

The foundation of understanding is the
willingness to listen.

Lord, fill my mouth with worthwhile stuff
and nudge me when I've said enough!

Charlie W. Shedd

The greatest obstacle to happiness is to expect
too much happiness.

Bernard le Bovier de Fontenelle

In sharing your fears with each other both of
you will become bolder; when sharing your
losses you will become richer; in sharing your
mistakes you will become wiser; and in sharing
yourselves you will become as one.

Remember that no matter how thin
you slice it, there are always two sides.

Ideals are like stars; you will not succeed in
touching them with your hands. But like
seafaring man on the desert of waters, you
choose them as your guides, and following
them you will reach your destiny.

Carl Schulz

Never eat more than you can lift.

Miss Piggy

Someone once said: Criticism never
built a house, wrote a play, composed a song,
painted a picture, or improved a marriage.

Never do anything in the first year of your
married life that you do not want to do the rest
of your life.   *Naomi Fuller Worsley*

It is because we are so different
from each other
that we have so much to share.

A wedding wish–
May you never forget
what is worth remembering
or remember
what is best forgotten

Irish

May you have the hindsight to know where
you've been...The foresight to know where
you're going...and the insight to know when
you've gone too far!   *Charles M. Meyers*

May the most the both of you wish for be the least the two of you receive.

Make the very most of all you've got and make the very least of what you can not get.

A story told by a rough old sheepherder in Colorado:

When a pack of fierce dogs plunder, or the coyotes come, there is one all-important difference between wild horses and wild asses. According to his account, when these deadly foes attack, the wild horses put their heads together in a tight center, tails to the windward side, and PROCEED TO KICK THE DEVIL OUT OF THEIR ADVERSARIES. But, if we can believe his reporting, when the wild asses are put upon, they place their heads toward the enemy, their tails to the inside, and THEY KICK THE DEVIL OUT OF EACH OTHER.

The lesson to be learned from this story for marriage: It is not what happens in a marriage that is so important as what you do with what happens.
Charlie W. Shedd

Occasions for Traditional Toasting

The Engagement Party: After the guests have assembled, the father of the bride proposes a toast to his daughter. Her fiancé, the groom answers with a toast to the bride and her family; other toasts follow.

Bachelor's Party: The groom presents the toast and everyone raises his glass to the bride with some going so far as to break the glass so that it may never be used for a less worthy cause.

Bachelorette Party: The bride proposes a toast to the groom and everyone raises her glass.

Rehersal Dinner: First, is the customary salute to the couple by the best man. The groom then follows with a toast to the bride and his new in-laws; then the bride toasts the groom and his family. Others may follow as they wish.

Reception: The wedding toast is traditionally given by the best man. He talks of how you both met and a few words about the hopes you have for your future. At the end of the toast he riases his glass and toasts to you, all guests raise their glass and join in the toast. You place your arm through the groom's and both drink. The locking of arms signifies the intertwining of your new lives. The groom may then respond by thanking the best man and toasting the bride, his new in-laws and his parents. The bride then adds her own toast honoring the groom and his family and thanking her parents.

Speeches

Marriage & Commitment

Divine wedlock: It has been described as two people growing both individually and in unity until they become what they were meant to be together. That is my wish for both of you–that you may reach your greatest heights together, committed to each other and to your marriage.

I like the way the president of a large university illustrates marriage. He says it is more than sharing each other's home, money, and children. It is the inner conviction that all roads lead home. Some days are going to be more difficult than others, but if you leave the airplane's escape hatch open because you think even before take-off that you may want to bail out in mid-flight, then I can assure you it is going to be a pretty chilly trip in less than fifteen minutes after leaving the ground. To make a marriage fly, close the door, strap on those seat belts, and give it a full throttle.

This same college president relates an experience when he was first married. He and his wife put everything they owned into their car, headed to a large university–two nameless, faceless, meaningless undergraduates–seeking their place in the sun. Before school started, they walked near the president's house when the student became completely overwhelmed with the challenge of a new marriage, new life, new education, no money, and no confidence. Turning to his new bride and fighting back the tears, he asked, "Do you think we can do this, have we made a mistake, should we withdraw? Can we compete with all of these people who know so much more than we do and are so capable?"

And then he said, "I guess that was the first time I saw what I would see again and again in her: the love, the confidence, the staying power, the careful handling of my fears." She must have been terrified herself, but she said, "Of course, we can do it!" But, you know, what is the best part of that story? Years later when he was president of that university, they would stand on the south patio of the president's home and look at exactly the same spot where two frightened students had stood fighting back the tears. He said they would stand there on days that had been most challenging and remember. He didn't say everything scary and hard went away with the years. There were days of still feeling fearful, but they had closed the door, strapped on the seat belt, and given it a full throttle.

Love is like that. It will temper and refine us, but it will not consume us. Marriage will temper and refine us, and take us to the greatest heights if we will let it.

May yours touch the stars.

Judy Macfarlane

Remember to Play in the Dirt

I am going to give you a bit of homey advice that may appear unusual at this time of satin and lace and formal attire. But I want you to think about this from time to time.

I am going to talk to you as you marry and think of happiness and families and success. I am going to tell you how important it is to *play in the dirt* and to remind you that he who plays in the dirt does so hand in hand with God.

By dirt, I mean the *soil*. That which is the rich black earth that can be found as close as your own backyard.

The earth has for all time given us our sustenance–grains and fruits and the beauty of flowers. The earth has also always given men and women a wonderful outlet, if they would only realize it. An outlet that is something productive for them to do with their hands, an outlet that is rich in a variety of rewards.

In a world grown increasingly mental and manipulative, not enough time or credit is given to just plain old-fashioned digging in the dirt. Our grandparents used to do it. We loved doing it as children. And, somehow, as adults in an overactive world, we have forgotten how to do it.

It doesn't matter if the dirt you choose to play in is found in only one small flower pot, a window box or a garden as big as your whole backyard. The time spent with your fingers in Mother Earth will give you a balance and an appreciation that just may make you calmer, a bit more reasonable, a lot more humble and a better human being. Remember that one is nearer God's heart in a garden than anywhere else on earth.

The real bottom line here is to play in the dirt and play in it *together*. What the two of you dig, what you plant, and what you harvest may be much more than you anticipate.

This same earth that gives so many things in life may play an important part in your relationship as the two of you remind yourselves that this small handful of dirt is the foundation of all growing things. It is alive and meant for things to grow within it. It is what William Lawson referred to as Paradise. It is a garden or an orchard of tress and herbs, both of which are full of pleasure and nothing but delights. "What", he asks, "can your eye desire to see, your nose to smell, your mouth to take that is not to be had in a garden?"

It is not the most profound thought ever offered, but I think it is pretty "well-grounded" advice. Play in the dirt, make a little garden out of life and walk contentedly down the path.

May the father of all dirt bless this union.

Michael Macfarlane

How To Be a Successful Speaker

If you plan to speak in public, regardless of how brief the speech or toast is to be, cultivate the art; inform yourself on your subject and present your thoughts briefly, clearly, with a smile upon your face, and a most sincere heart.

To be a successful speaker, here are a few suggestions that are good to know:

1. The first and most important rule is to be brief. The man or woman who has "a message to deliver" need only speak a few simple words of human interest to be assured he/she will never lack an audience.

2. The success of a speech on any occasion depends on whether the speaker has something to say, or whether you merely have to say something.

3. Be careful of too flamboyant an oratory style. Shakespeare advises: "Do not saw the air too much with your hands." Unless a gesture helps to emphasize your idea, it is best to omit it. If the words of the speaker are easy and their expression is pleasant, this is all that is needed by the audience.

4. Make your voice clear and easily heard.

5. Be careful not to talk above the heads of your audience.

6. If your speech is of the after-dinner variety, it must not contain too much wisdom. Your audience expects to be entertained, not instructed.

7. Deliver your words in a way that is most comfortable to you. If you can be seen by everyone in the room, you may stay seated.

8. Be prepared. If you know you are a likely candidate to give a speech or short toast, memorize or write a few ideas down before you arrive at the festivities.

9. Make certain that the toast or speech you are delivering is appropriate to the group.

10. Remember, you are the center of attention while speaking. Not only your words, but your appearance, expression, and attitude are on display. Remember, too, that you are a friend who was asked to share a very special moment and that one of the most popular toasts of all time was written for you alone: "Lord, fill my mouth with worthwhile stuff and nudge me when I've said enough!"

Index